THE LANGUAGE OF DREAMS

by

Cindy Loggins Hale

Third Edition

Cover art by Marilyn M. Hollon

Keithley Creek Publishing, LLC
Midvale, Idaho

Published by:
Keithley Creek Publishing, LLC
2275 Keithley Creek Road
Midvale, ID 83645

keithleycreek@gmail.com

www.keithleycreek.com

Visit our website or email us for more information about author speakers.

Print: 978-1-7322412-3-7
eBook: 978-1-7322412-6-8

Copyright © 2017 by C. L. Hale
Third edition Copyright ©2018 by Cindy Loggins Hale

All rights reserved, including the right to reproduce this book or portions thereof in any form whatsoever. All quotes and sources used by permission.

The information offered by Cindy Loggins Hale is neither made, provided, approved nor endorsed by Intellectual Reserve, Inc. or The Church of Jesus Christ of Latter-day Saints. Any content or opinions expressed, implied or included in or with the information offered by Cindy Loggins Hale are solely those of Cindy Loggins Hale and not those of Intellectual Reserve, Inc. or The Church of Jesus Christ of Latter-day Saints.

Distributed by:

Ingram Content Group, Inc.
One Ingram Blvd.
La Vergne, TN 37086

Printed and bound in United States by Ingram Spark

For my dear parents, Ira and Noretta Loggins,
who encouraged me to dream

TABLE OF CONTENTS

Introduction..7

Section 1: What do the Scriptures Say About Dreams?..15
How I Learned About Dreams...............................16

Prophetic Dreams
Joseph: Genesis 37..18
Joseph: Genesis 41..22
Isaac: Genesis 28..25
Gideon: Judges 7..27
Daniel & **Nebuchadnezzar:** Daniel 2 & 4...............29

Dreams of Warning or Instruction
The Wise Men & **Joseph:** Matthew 2......................37
Peter: Acts 10..40
Abimelech: Genesis 20..42
Lehi: 1 Nephi..44

Dreams Offering Problem Resolution
Pilate's Wife: Matthew 27:19.................................52
Omer: Ether 9...54
Jacob: Genesis 31..55

Dreams Offering Comfort

Joseph: Matthew 1..59

Solomon: 1 Kings 3..61

Section 2:
The Interpretation Process.......................63

Step 1: Preparing to Interpret Your Dreams.............65

Prepare Continually...66

Understand Your Role..70

Step 2: Record the Dream and Your Perspective.......76

Step 3: Understand the Significance of Symbols.......79

Step 4: Prayerfully Choose Your Interpretation.........84

Step 5: Access the Atonement of Jesus Christ..........91

INTRODUCTION

The following dream and its fulfillment, among many like it, have made me increasingly aware of the priceless gift that dreams can be. These experiences have taught me to listen, and given me cause to pay attention, when an unusual dream comes along. This book has come about because you and others are interested in how you can interpret your own dreams. I hope you may learn a few things and avoid my mistakes by reading it.

I awoke one morning from a very satisfying but perplexing dream. In it I was driving our old car on a beautiful sunny day, with my children in the back seat. I was headed west on a busy highway in my hometown in Southern California. I came to a place where the road divided. On the left was the cemetery where many of my family members are buried. While the place had once had some pleasant associations, such as family memories and cute animals we spied when decorating the graves, it appeared now as a dark, dank, ugly place. The place smelled terrible.

For some reason my husband (at the time) was hanging around the area, down a short gravel road near some half-dead trees, and was unwilling to go anywhere else. To the right was an open road, heading north. It appeared pleasant, but I could not see the end of this road. The light changed, and I had to decide which way to turn, as stopping there was not an option. I could see the end of the road that turned south into the cemetery, and it didn't look appealing. So, on this bright, glorious morning, my children and I headed north.

The drive was pleasant, but the distance was long, and the day waned. Towards sunset I saw a billboard with a Book of Mormon and a Temple on it. That was significant to me; you normally don't see those in my hometown. The billboard indicated some event up ahead. We went a little further and there was a little valley where people were gathered. There were hot-air balloons and people were dancing in red, green, black and white folk costumes. There were various pickup trucks and horse trailers parked on the dusty ground. Sagebrush grew on the surrounding land. All around us I saw golden hills and an intensely clear, bright blue sky. Growing up in my hometown, clear blue skies were an increasing rarity due to the prevalence of smog, smoke and haze in such a heavily-populated area, so that detail was memorable. We stopped in this valley as the sun began to set, and were very happy. I awoke feeling such peace and a profound calm. I also had the persistent and overwhelming feeling that this dream was very important.

This dream occurred more than twenty years ago during a relatively happy, stable period in my life. My marriage and family meant everything to me, and I took great joy in teaching my children and learning from my experiences. I did not understand the dream's significance at the time, but this dream was unusually vivid, enough to prompt me to write it down and think about it.

Over the years, I have come to realize that this dream was prophetic. Remembering the dream's journey offered a lasting and ongoing comfort to me as devastating changes occurred in my life that shook me to my foundations, and nearly undid me mentally. I came to a great spiritual crossroads, and was faced with a momentous choice and a cross-country move. The details in the latter part of my dream stood as markers in my journey, and have signified to me when I was where the Lord wanted me to be. They enabled me over the years to take bold action at times I otherwise might have cowered in fear.

The full interpretation of this dream did not become apparent until many years had passed, although I increasingly began seeing the parallels to what was happening in my life. Following are some of the markers along the way that helped me see that the dream was the Lord's way of tenderly blessing me with comfort and strength:

- Within a few years immediately following the dream, my cherished marriage disintegrated into ashes, despite all my efforts to the contrary. I was directed in prayer during this horrible, stressful process to move to Idaho. This was unexpected and highly unusual under the circumstances. My request was met with disbelief and disapproval from my attorney and the court at first. In the long months of waiting between court dates, I was able to volunteer at the Open House for a new temple, dedicated just eight miles from where I grew up. It was an object of fascination in the community and many discussions revolved around it, even in court.

•Just a month after the Temple was dedicated, I was miraculously given sole custody of our three minor children and allowed to move wherever I wished. My father and mother decided to sell their home of 38 years and move to Idaho as well, to help me. The scene of turning north and leaving the scene of spiritual death became a literal reality. During this time, I often drew courage from the life of Nephi, a prophet in the Book of Mormon, who left a scene of spiritual death in his hometown and family life, and found safety in a new land.

•Within a year of our arrival, Boise, Idaho was the scene of Jaialdi, a special Basque festival occurring only once every five years. I had never heard of this festival, or Idaho's considerable Basque population, before our arrival. I was amazed at television reports of this festival, where I saw the same dancers, dressed in the same red, white, green and black costumes as in my dream many years before. That was striking to me.

•Another sign appeared a few years later. While

driving early one morning through Boise as part of my job, a breathtaking sight appeared of numerous hot air balloons rising from the fairgrounds, exactly as I had seen in the dream.

• A period of two or three years went by, during which time we were fairly well provided for, with a job, friends, and family nearby, just as in the long but pleasant road we traveled in the dream.

• When a new Temple was announced for Twin Falls, Idaho, just 125 miles away, I began to see new parallels in the dream to what was going on around me, and began to wonder where it all would lead.

• In the beginning of 2008, a renewed emphasis on the Book of Mormon occurred throughout our church as part of the four-year rotation of scripture study. The Twin Falls Temple was dedicated later that year.

• I met a wonderful man that in July 2008. The following year, he and I married - happily. This event brought a lot of personal joy, but other trials came along, as they regularly do. A surprising, distressing loss of my job within a couple of years made us unable to pay for the home in the suburbs. We moved to a small town nearby where my husband had a house. We moved over the period of a month, using a friend's trailer, in order to save money. One afternoon, several weeks into the move, I was driving one of the last trailer loads of our belongings. We had made countless trips, and I was exhausted. I drove a different route than usual, to avoid the heavy late-afternoon rush-hour traffic. The road I took went up into the hills, from an area I was familiar with into winding roads I had never traveled before. I didn't know exactly how things would work out, but knew the general direction I needed to go, and according to a map I checked we would come out in the right place. I just had to get away from the crowded, anxiety-ridden highway. Driving through the hills, sometimes on dirt roads, I was astounded to realize that around me were scenes very similar to the last of my dream, with the golden hills and bright blue sky, even a small gathering of dusty ranchers' trucks. Seeing these things profoundly confirmed the rightness of our move. I felt comforted in my distress and exhaustion, and began to look forward to the future. We settled in happily at the house, located in a small housing subdivision.

•After about a year, the opportunity came to serve a full-time mission for our church, something we had not even considered at our former location. A couple in our congregation agreed to live in and care for our home and pets, which was a great blessing. My husband and I spent a wonderful 19 months together serving in Pennsylvania. When we returned in 2014, however, I felt restless. It seemed that our home and its surroundings no longer fit us. As I prayed about what to do, the feeling came to me that when the time was right, we should go **NORTH**. We both felt good about that but did nothing.

•We finally started looking at homes in the fall of 2015, but could not find anything suitable in the little town we lived in. We spent some time in the Temple, thinking perhaps the restlessness would subside, but it increased tenfold in intensity. Extending our search online, we found a place online located north and west of us, far out in the country, a tiny town in a land of tiny towns. We went to see this home, and as we approached it, driving into a small rural valley surrounded by steeply sloped, enormous golden hills and deep, brilliant blue skies, I was again reminded of the happy little valley foretold in the dream long ago. The expansive view made the place quiver with potential, and we felt immediate relief from the pressing restlessness that had gone on so long. So we bought the house.

•Here I have found the peace, happiness and solitude I needed to heal mentally and physically and do things the Lord has asked me to do - including writing this book. As I look west from my home and barn, I see the final scene from my dream, right down to the dusty pickups and horse trailers, surrounded by those golden hills and blue skies. I have found the place where I belong. And indeed, I am happy here, after all the struggles. We are both at peace in this country life.

    Knowing the desires of my heart, and knowing my efforts to make progress despite challenges, the Lord sent a dream to help me through what would be a very difficult journey. Because of the dream, I held onto hope that I would someday find a place where I could express myself fully. This dream is just one example of many of how the Lord has taught me how dreams work.

    You likely have experienced dreams that seem to bear an important message to you, and you want to understand them better. It is my hope that, as you read on, you will find the help you need, and become able to receive, hear and understand all the messages of help, comfort, and instruction the Lord is sending you through the beautiful, symbolic and miraculous language of dreams.

C. L. Hale

Section I:
What do the scriptures say about inspired dreams?

How I learned about dreams

When I was a young mother, perhaps 25 years old, I recall being instructed in prayer to write a talk and start carrying it and my scriptures with me to our weekly church meetings. I spent time writing out my thoughts, and it evolved into a discourse on inspired dreams. I never actually delivered this as a speech, but over the years have continued thinking about the subject of dreams. I often had dreams, sometimes elaborate, detailed ones, but usually did not understand their meaning. I found some words by Sterling W Sill inspiring when contemplating the subject, when he told of a dream he had as a young man about doing calisthenics on a field with other men. Several years later, after entering military service, he found himself in the very circumstance of his dream - and not as a particularly enjoyable experience. He realized only much later the volume of instruction he might have had, and how his path might have been different, if he had applied himself to interpreting the dream early on. So I began studying the scriptures as they relate to dream interpretation.

The following section comprises a discussion of scripture stories dealing with dreams. While we do not know zll the specifics of each dream situation, each instance given involves interpretation of a dream, with its application to real life, and makes clear certain things about the process of interpreting dreams. The stories are arranged by dream type.

PROPHETIC DREAMS

Joseph – Genesis 37

Perhaps the most famous and dramatic story of dream interpretation in all of Scripture, Genesis 37:5-15 tells the story of Joseph's first inspired dreams.

Joseph's brothers hated him because he was favored by his father as the first son of Rachel, his father's first love. Joseph "dreamed a dream", and told it to his brothers: "For, behold, we were binding sheaves in the field, and, lo, my sheaf arose, and also stood upright; and, behold, your sheaves stood round about, and made obeisance to my sheaf."

Joseph was young, and perhaps made a slight error in judgment, not understanding the depth of their resentment towards him. His brothers did not react well: "And his brethren said to him, Shalt thou indeed reign over us? or shalt thou indeed have dominion over us? And they hated him yet the more for his dreams, and for his words".

The theme of the dream was repeated in a second dream, which Joseph told his brothers, "Behold, I have dreamed a dream more; and, behold, the sun and the moon and the eleven stars made obeisance to me."

This time, when he told his father and his brothers, his father rebuked him, saying "What is this dream that thou hast dreamed? Shall I and thy mother and thy brethren indeed come to bow down ourselves to thee to the earth? And his brethren envied him; but his father observed the saying."

The record does not say a lot about the actual process of Joseph's coming to an interpretation of these first dreams. Certainly his trials led to increased prayer and reliance upon God's comfort, and taking an eternal viewpoint when considering the path of his life. Joseph's stewardship to his family regarding the dream was fulfilled as he informed them of it. Soon thereafter, his life took a tumultuous turn.

Within the space of just a few years, Joseph was sold into slavery, taken far out of his own land into Egypt, and set up in the nobleman Potiphar's house. Soon thereafter he was falsely accused and then imprisoned. Prison alone would have given Joseph a lot of time to think. He must have wondered and prayed a great deal about his first dreams, seeking help and comfort in all of the irony and sorrows that had befallen him.

Not long after Joseph was placed in prison, he got to know some of his fellow prisoners. The Pharaoh's butler and baker had each offended their master and were imprisoned; they happened to be in the same area as Joseph. In one night, both of these men had a dream. In his regular duties as assistant to the head prison guard, Joseph checked on the men in the morning. They were sad, and he asked them what was wrong. They said: "We have dreamed a dream, and there is no interpreter of it." Joseph answered: "Do not interpretations belong to God? tell me them, I pray you."

The butler told his dream: "In my dream, behold, a vine was before me; And in the vine were three branches: and it was as though it budded, and her blossoms shot forth; and the clusters thereof brought forth ripe grapes: And Pharaoh's cup was in my hand: and I took the grapes, and pressed them into Pharaoh's cup, and I gave the cup into Pharaoh's hand."

Because of his spiritual readiness, Joseph immediately understood the interpretation, which he shared: "This is the interpretation of it: The three branches are three days: Yet within three days shall Pharaoh lift up thine head, and restore thee unto thy place: and thou shalt deliver Pharaoh's cup into his hand, after the former manner when thou wast his butler." Joseph then immediately asked the butler to remember him to Pharaoh, and assured him of his innocence of any wrongdoing. Joseph's faith in the interpretation gave him confidence to make that request.

The baker, hearing such an encouraging interpretation, told Joseph his dream: "I also was in my dream, and, behold, I had three white baskets on my head: And in the uppermost basket there was of all manner of bakemeats for Pharaoh; and the birds did eat them out of the basket upon my head."

Joseph's interpretation was quick in this case also, but not such good news for the baker: "This is the interpretation thereof: The three baskets are three days: Yet within three days shall Pharaoh lift up thy head from off thee, and shall hang thee on a tree; and the birds shall eat thy flesh from off thee." Three days later, both interpretations were proved correct. The butler, however, forgot about Joseph until the Pharaoh himself was troubled by inspired dreams.

Joseph – Genesis 41

Two full years later, Pharaoh dreamed that he stood by the river, and out from the river came up seven fat, well-favored cattle that walked over and fed in a meadow. Then seven other cattle came up after them out of the river, ugly and scrawny, and stood by the other cattle by the edge of the river. Then the ugly, scrawny cattle ate up the seven fat, well-favored cattle. So Pharaoh awoke. Soon he slept and dreamed the second time: seven ears of corn came up upon one stalk, full and good. Then seven thin ears, "blasted with the east wind, sprung up after them. And the seven thin ears devoured the seven rank and full ears." Pharaoh awoke.

In the morning "Pharaoh's spirit was troubled; and he sent and called for all the magicians of Egypt, and all the wise men thereof." Pharaoh told them about this dream, "but there was none that could interpret them unto Pharaoh," suggesting that perhaps these wise men and magicians offered personal interpretations and ideas – it was their job, after all. However, none of those interpretations felt right to Pharaoh, or satisfied the question created by the dream.

The butler, still in the Pharaoh's service, heard about the Pharaoh's dreams – and remembered his promise to Joseph. Joseph was brought in, and immediately upon hearing of the two dreams realized that they contained one message, that of the seven years of plenty and seven years of famine to come. He was filled with inspiration and knew just what needed to be done. Joseph's circumstances changed instantly as Pharaoh recognized the truth of the interpretation and Joseph's preparation to fulfill the needed position.

Things we can learn from Joseph about interpreting dreams:

- Inspired dreams may be troubling, to some degree.
- Sharing inspired dreams may not be a pleasant experience.
- Interpretations belong to God. To understand a true interpretation of your dream, it makes sense that you need to be doing your best to understand Him and His ways. Thus you need to:
    -Build a good spiritual foundation - seek Him in His Word.
    -Be worthy, and obedient to God's will.
    -Be faithful in what is entrusted to you (your stewardship).
    -Be prayerful.
    -Be humble.
    -Be patient.
- Correct interpretations satisfy the questions the dream evokes. They feel right, calm and balanced, whether or not you like the interpretation. Some-

times you realize you knew all along, but were looking for a different answer.
- A correct interpretation may take time and trial to understand. Keep looking.
- Dreams contain symbols that represent deeper meaning.
- Dreams may be prophetic of future events.
- Dreams may or may not contain welcome news.
- Dreams may invite action or change.

ISAAC – GENESIS 28

While traveling, Isaac, who slept alone in the desert with a rock for a pillow, had a dream of a ladder reaching into heaven - symbolizing his eternal journey. The ladder was "set up on the earth, and the top of it reached to heaven: and behold the angels of God ascending and descending on it."

13 And, behold, the Lord stood above it, and said, I am the Lord God of Abraham thy father, and the God of Isaac: the land whereon thou liest, to thee will I give it, and to thy seed;

14 And thy seed shall be as the dust of the earth, and thou shalt spread abroad to the west, and to the east, and to the north, and to the south: and in thee and in thy seed shall all the families of the earth be blessed.

15 And, behold, I am with thee, and will keep thee in all places whither thou goest, and will bring thee again into this land; for I will not leave thee, until I have done that which I have spoken to thee of.

A ladder is symbolic of higher responsibility and is an invitation to *climb higher* than one would normally. In Isaac's dream, it represented the covenant Isaac had made with God, and invited him to reach towards God with an even greater effort. It promised him that God would be with him. The dream implied higher levels and greater blessings in store as Isaac listened and obeyed.

Isaac was inspired and filled with joy and reverence. He then vowed obedience with regard to his tithes and worship.

Things we can learn from Isaac about interpreting dreams:

- The Lord's perspective encompasses all eternity. He sees us, even in our dire or discouraging circumstances, and helps us make forward progress despite challenges.
- Inspired dreams are meant to prepare us, to help us look upward and move forward in eternal progress.
- We can show our gratitude for inspired dreams by increasing our obedience and faithfulness.

GIDEON – JUDGES 7

Gideon, leader of the Army of Israel, was facing an innumerable enemy. As Gideon prayed for help, the Lord surprisingly directed him to reduce the Israelite Army from more than 32,000 men to only 300. Gideon was then commanded to lead the army down into the multitude of Midianites and Amalekites, and begin the battle, but he was afraid. The Lord told him to take his servant Phurah and go among them, to listen to what they were saying.

12 And the Midianites and the Amalekites and all the children of the east lay along in the valley like grasshoppers for multitude; and their camels were without number, as the sand by the sea side for multitude.
13 And when Gideon was come, behold, there was a man that told a dream unto his fellow, and said, Behold, I dreamed a dream, and, lo, a cake of barley bread tumbled into the host of Midian, and came unto a tent, and smote it that it fell, and overturned it, that the tent lay along.
14 And his fellow answered and said, This is nothing else save the sword of Gideon the son of Joash, a man of Israel: for into his hand hath God delivered Midian, and all the host.
15 And it was so, when Gideon heard the telling of the dream, and the interpretation thereof, that he worshipped, and returned into the host of Isra-

el, and said, Arise; for the Lord hath delivered into your hand the host of Midian.

The inspired dream in this case was not Gideon's, but by following the Spirit's direction, he was placed within hearing of this inspired dream. The dream was an encouragement to him, and also to his soldiers. Gideon instantly recognized the interpretation and its significance to the battle ahead. The 300 Israelite soldiers broke pottery and held up lamps when the trumpet to battle sounded in the night, and the innumerable host ran away, confused and terrified. The battle was over before it ever really began.

Things we can learn from Gideon about interpreting dreams:

- Learn to recognize and then follow the still, small voice of the Spirit in your daily life.
- The Lord can give you instruction, blessings and help from the most unexpected places.
- Trust that the Lord will help you fight the battles He asks you to take on.
- The Lord's ways are not the same as man's ways.

Daniel and Nebuchadnezzar – Daniel 2 & 4

Nebuchadnezzar, king of Babylon, subdued Jerusalem in 587 BC, and took many of the best and brightest children home with him as captives, including Daniel and three of his friends. The following year, the king began having dreams that troubled him. Nebuchanezzar called all his magicians, astrologers, sorcerers, and other counselors to help him. Ready and willing, they asked the king to tell them the dream. However, Nebuchadnezzar had forgotten the dream, having not written it down upon arising. He was still troubled by it, and insisted that these counselors use their "magic" to both tell him the dream and the interpretation of it.

These magicians and sorcerers professed a spiritual expertise that they could not really deliver, and Nebuchadnezzar was weary of it. He became angry, and said that unless they told him the dream *and* the interpretation, all of the wise men would be put to death. Daniel heard of the decree when the captain of the king's guard came to kill him.

Daniel asked that the king give him and his companions a little time, and they would give him the dream and interpretation. They prayed that they might be given the information they needed in order to preserve their lives. The dream was given to Daniel, along with the interpretation, in a night vision. He praised the Lord with all his heart, and sent word to the king that he had the information requested. When the king inquired, Daniel gave complete credit to the Lord.

Daniel then explained the interpretation of each of the dream's symbols, which, beginning with Nebuchadnezzar as the head of gold, listed in succession the kingdoms and dynasties that would follow his reign, even unto the time that God would set up His kingdom on the Earth. While this dream does not appear to have benefitted Nebuchadnezzar very much, it is of immense value to those trying to understand the purposes of God and His doings in later times.

37 Thou, O king, art a king of kings: for the God of heaven hath given thee a kingdom, power, and strength, and glory.

38 And wheresoever the children of men dwell, the beasts of the field and the fowls of the heaven hath he given into thine hand, and hath made thee ruler over them all. Thou art this head of gold.

39 And after thee shall arise another kingdom inferior to thee, and another third kingdom of brass, which shall bear rule over all the earth.

40 And the fourth kingdom shall be strong as iron: forasmuch as iron breaketh in pieces and subdueth all things: and as iron that breaketh all these, shall it break in pieces and bruise.

41 And whereas thou sawest the feet and toes, part of potters' clay, and part of iron, the kingdom shall be divided; but there shall be in it of the strength of the iron, forasmuch as thou sawest the iron mixed with miry clay.

42 And as the toes of the feet were part of iron, and part of clay, so the kingdom shall be partly strong, and partly broken.

43 And whereas thou sawest iron mixed with miry clay, they shall mingle themselves with the seed of men: but they shall not cleave one to another, even as iron is not mixed with clay.

44 And in the days of these kings shall the God of heaven set up a kingdom, which shall never be destroyed: and the kingdom shall not be left to other people, but it shall break in pieces and consume all these kingdoms, and it shall stand for ever.

45 Forasmuch as thou sawest that the stone was cut out of the mountain without hands, and that it brake in pieces the iron, the brass, the clay, the silver, and the gold; the great God hath made known to the king what shall come to pass hereafter: and the dream is certain, and the interpretation thereof sure.

Nebuchadnezzar's reaction to the dream, perhaps on the advisement of his astrologers, led to his making an enormous gold statue or idol, which all of the people were expected to worship. Daniel and his friends Shadrach, Meshach and Abednego refused to worship it, and Shadrach, Meshach and Abednego were cast into the fiery furnace. They miraculously survived. When the king could not deny that their God had delivered them from sure death, he changed his tune and allowed their freedom of worship. Nebuchadnezzar made a public proclamation praising Daniel (whom he called Belteshazzar) and his friends, and their God. However, his persistent pride resulted in a humbling end.

Nebuchadnezzar then had another dream, one that contained meaning more personal to himself. He dreamed of a great tree "in the midst of the earth" that was of great height, and grew tall and strong. It reached to heaven, and was visible to all the ends of the earth. It had beautiful leaves, and much fruit that fed "all flesh" including beasts of the field that took refuge in its shade and fowls that lived in its branches.

13 I saw in the visions of my head upon my bed, and, behold, a watcher and an holy one came down from heaven;

14 He cried aloud, and said thus, Hew down the tree, and cut off his branches, shake off his leaves, and scatter his fruit: let the beasts get away from under it, and the fowls from his branches:

15 Nevertheless leave the stump of his roots in the earth, even with a band of iron and brass, in the tender grass of the field; and let it be wet with the dew of heaven, and let his portion be with the beasts in the grass of the earth:

16 Let his heart be changed from man's, and let a beast's heart be given unto him; and let seven times pass over him.

17 This matter is by the decree of the watchers, and the demand by the word of the holy ones: to the intent that the living may know that the most High ruleth in the kingdom of men, and giveth it to whomsoever he will, and setteth up over it the basest of men.

Nebuchadnezzar finished describing his dream, and asked Daniel to interpret it, stating that the "wise men of the kingdom" were not able to help him with it. He expressed faith that Daniel would understand it, saying "thou art able; for the spirit of the holy gods is in thee". Daniel understood the interpretation of the dream readily enough, but found himself in the unenviable position of having to give unpleasant news to a prideful king. However, after assurance from the king that he need not fear, he did so:

19 Then Daniel, whose name was Belteshazzar, was astonied for one hour, and his thoughts troubled him. The king spake, and said, Belteshazzar, let not the dream, or the interpretation thereof, trouble thee. Belteshazzar answered and said, My lord, the dream be to them that hate thee, and the interpretation thereof to thine enemies.

20 The tree that thou sawest, which grew, and was strong, whose height reached unto the heaven, and the sight thereof to all the earth;

21 Whose leaves were fair, and the fruit thereof much, and in it was meat for all; under which the beasts of the field dwelt, and upon whose branches the fowls of the heaven had their habitation:

22 It is thou, O king, that art grown and become strong: for thy greatness is grown, and reacheth unto heaven, and thy dominion to the end of the earth.

23 And whereas the king saw a watcher and an holy one coming down from heaven, and saying, Hew the tree down, and destroy it; yet leave the stump of the roots thereof in the earth, even with a band of iron and brass, in the tender grass of the field; and let it be wet with the dew of heaven, and let his portion be with the beasts of the field, till seven times pass over him;

24 This is the interpretation, O king, and this is the decree of the most High, which is come upon my lord the king:

25 That they shall drive thee from men, and thy dwelling shall be with the beasts of the field, and they shall make thee to eat grass as oxen, and they shall wet thee with the dew of heaven, and seven times shall pass over thee, till thou know that the most High ruleth in the kingdom of men, and giveth it to whomsoever he will.

26 And whereas they commanded to leave the stump of the tree roots; thy kingdom shall be sure unto thee, after that thou shalt have known that the heavens do rule.

27 Wherefore, O king, let my counsel be acceptable unto thee, and break off thy sins by righteousness, and thine iniquities by shewing mercy to the poor; if it may be a lengthening of thy tranquillity.

King Nebuchadnezzar was counseled to repent, be humble and offer mercy to the poor, in order to prolong his peaceful existence. The interpretation did come to pass about one year later. As the king was actually in the act of praising himself, his mental state swiftly deteriorated to the point that he was found crawling on the ground, eating grass. The kingdom then passed to his son Belshazzar.

Things we can learn from Daniel and Nebuchadnezzar:
- Inspired dreams come from the Lord's eternal perspective. Nebuchadnezzar was unable to humble himself sufficiently, so the Lord changed his circumstances so he would learn humility. This lesson was not necessarily punishment, but it was important to his eternal progress.
- Be careful not to let praise go to your head. You are but one cog in one gear in the enormous mechanism of God's Kingdom on the earth. Give credit to the Lord and avoid pride.
- It is important to write dreams down. A dream that comes to you might be for the benefit and understanding of people far removed from you. In our present day we can see the beginning of the fulfillment of Nebuchadnezzar's dream, many thousand years later. It is wonderful that Daniel recorded it, and that it has been preserved all this time. The Lord's perspective is immense.

Dreams of Warning or Instruction

The Wise Men and Joseph –Matthew 2

Under inspiration from God, wise men came to see the baby Jesus, and were prepared with gifts for Him. They talked with the ruler of Judea, King Herod, but a vicious jealousy consumed him when he heard about prophecies of another king. The wise men were given a message in a dream that they should not return to Herod. They heeded the warning, even though it put their own lives at risk:

> **11** And when they were come into the house, they saw the young child with Mary his mother, and fell down, and worshipped him: and when they had opened their treasures, they presented unto him gifts; gold, and frankincense, and myrrh.
>
> **12** And being warned of God in a dream that they should not return to Herod, they departed into their own country another way.

Immediately thereafter, Joseph, husband of Mary, was also given a dream to protect baby Jesus. Joseph acted immediately upon the instruction given him:

> **13** And when they were departed, behold, the angel of the Lord appeareth to Joseph in a dream, saying, Arise, and take the young child and his mother, and flee into Egypt, and be thou there un-

til I bring thee word: for Herod will seek the young child to destroy him.

14 When he arose, he took the young child and his mother by night, and departed into Egypt:

Things we can learn from Joseph and the Wise Men about interpreting dreams:

- Heed the warning you receive, even if it involves risk.
- Act immediately upon clear promptings to action.

Peter – Acts 10

As a new prophet, Peter was particularly careful to teach only truth, and to lead in righteousness. One day during a journey, Peter was tired and hungry, but the Lord chose that particular time to teach Peter an important lesson:

9 On the morrow, as they went on their journey, and drew nigh unto the city, Peter went up upon the housetop to pray about the sixth hour:

10 And he became very hungry, and would have eaten: but while they made ready, he fell into a trance,

11 And saw heaven opened, and a certain vessel descending unto him, as it had been a great sheet knit at the four corners, and let down to the earth:

12 Wherein were all manner of fourfooted beasts of the earth, and wild beasts, and creeping things, and fowls of the air.

13 And there came a voice to him, Rise, Peter; kill, and eat.

14 But Peter said, Not so, Lord; for I have never eaten any thing that is common or unclean.

15 And the voice spake unto him again the second time, What God hath cleansed, that call not thou common.

Peter, through an inspired dream, was given new direction for the Saints of his time. This direction radically differed from the cultural norms of the day, which prescribed a clearly separate existence between believers and non-believers. Peter was instructed to take the Gospel to the Gentiles, whom the Jews had traditionally shunned in their business and personal dealings.

Things we can learn from Peter about interpreting inspired dreams:

- The Lord may use your current circumstances to teach you something abstract. In hindsight, you may find that the lesson may be the only reason you are in the situation at all.
- Be open to the possibility of change, and a paradigm shift.
- Be willing to go against the tide of public opinion and tradition, when so directed by the Lord.

Abimelech – Genesis 20

Abraham, seeking relief from famine, headed for Egypt. He and his wife Sarah traveled through Gerar, located in the south-central part of present-day Israel.

Abraham was warned by the Lord to tell those he met in his travels that Sarah was his sister. This was not entirely untrue, as Sarah was the daughter of Abraham's brother. The Philistine culture of the time made it safer to be a brother of a beautiful woman, someone to be persuaded for her hand, than to be her husband, someone to dispose of quickly so that she would become a marriageable widow. Abraham was obedient, and called Sarah his sister on this trip.

Abimelech, the Philistine king of Gerar, admired Sarah, and wanted to marry her. He separated Abraham and Sarah, and attempted to make her his wife, but things did not work out as he planned. God "came to Abimelech in a dream by night, and said to him, Behold, thou art but a dead man, for the woman which thou hast taken; for she is a man's wife."

4 But Abimelech had not come near her: and he said, Lord, wilt thou slay also a righteous nation?

5 Said he not unto me, She is my sister? and she, even she herself said, He is my brother: in the integrity of my heart and innocency of my hands have I done this.

6 And God said unto him in a dream, Yea, I know that thou didst this in the integrity of thy heart; for I also withheld thee from sinning against me: therefore suffered I thee not to touch her.

7 Now therefore restore the man his wife; for he is a prophet, and he shall pray for thee, and thou shalt live: and if thou restore her not, know thou that thou shalt surely die, thou, and all that are thine.

Abimelech quickly restored Sarah to Abraham, and sent them on their way. Abimelech was given some concrete boundaries in the dream, and wisdom to move forward. Abraham also learned from this experience that Abimelech was worthy enough to have an inspired dream.

Things we can learn from Abraham and Abimelech about interpreting dreams:

- Be willing to admit you were wrong.
- Trust that the Lord has your best interests at heart.
- What you want may not always be what is best for you.
- Allow the Lord to teach you and others through dreams.

Lehi – 1 Nephi

Lehi's calling as a prophet gave him stewardship over many people in addition to his own family. As a result, he wrote "many things which he saw in visions and in dreams; and he also hath written many things which he prophesied and spake unto his children ."

One of Lehi's first dreams recorded in the Book of Mormon warned him to leave Jerusalem, where the powerful were intent on killing him, angry because he had prophesied their destruction, as instructed by the Lord.

1 Nephi 2:1 For behold, it came to pass that the Lord spake unto my father, yea, even in a dream, and said unto him: Blessed art thou Lehi, because of the things which thou hast done; and because thou hast been faithful and declared unto this people the things which I commanded thee, behold, they seek to take away thy life.

2 And it came to pass that the Lord commanded my father, even in a dream, that he should take his family and depart into the wilderness.

3 And it came to pass that he was obedient unto the word of the Lord, wherefore he did as the Lord commanded him.

The next dream came to Lehi for the benefit of all people. It told him to obtain the scriptures from Laban, likely Lehi's relative and certainly the current guardian over the records in Jerusalem:

1 Nephi 3: 2 And it came to pass that he spake unto me, saying: Behold I have dreamed a dream, in the which the Lord hath commanded me that thou and thy brethren shall return to Jerusalem.

3 For behold, Laban hath the record of the Jews and also a genealogy of my forefathers, and they are engraven upon plates of brass.

4 Wherefore, the Lord hath commanded me that thou and thy brothers should go unto the house of Laban, and seek the records, and bring them down hither into the wilderness.

Nephi's faithfulness to his father and to the Lord in believing and acting upon this dream blessed him, his whole family, as well as all of his people in succeeding generations. It inspires even us in the present day. Nephi's obedience also gained him an ally in Laban's servant Zoram, who was certainly a strength to him as he faced his brothers' rebellion and murderous threats.

1 Nephi 8 describes a third dream or vision that Lehi experienced, a wonderful one that contains im-

portant symbolism applicable to every individual.

In the dream, he saw a man, who asked Lehi to follow him through a dark and dreary wasteland. After many hours of travel, Lehi prayed for help in crossing this miserable place, and he saw a large and spacious field. In the field he saw a tree that bore fruit that was the key to happiness. He tasted the fruit, and it was the sweetest, purest, most wonderful experience ever. It filled him with happiness, and he wanted his family to be able to partake of it.

Lehi saw his wife and sons far off, and called to them to eat. Sariah, Nephi and Sam came and ate of the fruit, but Laman and Lemuel would not. Lehi saw a rod of iron leading to the tree alongside a river, and a straight and narrow path that ran next to it. The rod passed also the fountain where the river of water originated.

Crowds of people were traveling through this area, and dark mists arose, obscuring their way. Those who held onto the rod were able to get to the tree and enjoy its fruit. Those who let go fell into the filthy river. Others came by way of the path and the iron rod, and partook of the fruit, but looked around, ashamed.

A great and spacious building was situated nearby, where multitudes of well-dressed people were pointing and laughing at those who partook of the wonderful fruit of the tree. Some of those who had tasted this wonderful fruit left the tree, "fell into forbidden paths and were lost." Many sought the spacious building, which they could not reach.

Nephi spent much time in prayer, seeking to understand his father's dream. He sought to understand each symbol as it pertained to the whole. In answer to his prayer, he was not only shown the meaning of specific symbols from the dream, but shown the dream in its entirety. Chapters 11 to 15 describe a wonderful outpouring of the Spirit in prophetic vision that came to Nephi as a result of his faithful desire to understand.

As he returned to his tent from receiving all of this instruction, he found his brothers arguing about the meaning of their father's dream, and they asked him pointedly what it meant. Unlike Nephi, they were unwilling to seek the Lord in prayer themselves. Nephi, though burdened, grieved and exhausted by all he had seen, including the eventual destruction of his entire posterity, patiently answered their questions.

Laman and Lemuel asked him, "What meaneth this thing which our father saw in a dream? What meaneth the tree which he saw? And Nephi replied that it "was a representation of the tree of life." They asked further, "What meaneth the rod of iron which our father saw, that led to the tree?" To which Nephi responded that "it was the word of God; and whoso would hearken unto the word of God, and would hold fast unto it, they would never perish; neither could the temptations and the fiery darts of the adversary overpower them unto blindness, to lead them away to destruction." Nephi then asked them to pay attention to the words of God, with all the strength and energy he possessed:

> **1 Nephi 15:25** Wherefore, I, Nephi, did exhort them to give heed unto the word of the Lord; yea, I did exhort them with all the energies of my soul, and with all the faculty which I possessed, that they would give heed to the word of God and remember to keep his commandments always in all things.

Laman and Lemuel, however, seemed more interested in quizzing or testing Nephi for their own curiosity than in seeking out any answers for themselves. Nephi's patience in this situation is exemplary.

> **26** And they said unto me: What meaneth the river of water which our father saw?

> **27** And I said unto them that the water which my father saw was filthiness; and so much was his mind swallowed up in other things that he beheld not the filthiness of the water.

28 And I said unto them that it was an awful gulf, which separated the wicked from the tree of life, and also from the saints of God.

29 And I said unto them that it was a representation of that awful hell, which the angel said unto me was prepared for the wicked.

30 And I said unto them that our father also saw that the justice of God did also divide the wicked from the righteous; and the brightness thereof was like unto the brightness of a flaming fire, which ascendeth up unto God forever and ever, and hath no end.

The marvelous interpretation Nephi received came after exhaustive study coupled with sincere and powerful prayer and perfect obedience. He willingly shared his learning, but Laman and Lemuel had less appreciation for it, being unwilling to devote much personal effort or obedience to furthering their spiritual understanding.

Things we can learn about dream interpretation from Lehi and Nephi:

- Personal prayer and effort are important in discerning the meaning of inspired dreams. The Lord often waits for us to ask before He will enlighten us with an interpretation. Perhaps this is because once we

understand a thing, we are accountable for that knowledge.
- Attention to detail is vital in understanding the meaning of dreams.
- Persistent obedience to God enables the interpretation of prophetic dreams.
- Dreams that come through us may benefit untold generations after us.
- Patience is necessary with the interpretation process, both in receiving and individual interpretation, and, if needed, in teaching others about the understanding one has received.

Dreams Offering Problem Resolution

Pilate's wife – Matthew 27:19

The wife of Pilate, procurator of Jerusalem at the time of Jesus' crucifixion, received a warning in a dream the day of Jesus' trial:

17 Therefore when they were gathered together, Pilate said unto them, Whom will ye that I release unto you? Barabbas, or Jesus which is called Christ?

18 For he knew that for envy they had delivered him.

19 When he was set down on the judgment seat, his wife sent unto him, saying, Have thou nothing to do with that just man: for I have suffered many things this day in a dream because of him.

Perhaps it was because of the warning of his wife's dream that Pilate publicly washed his hands immediately after this point, symbolically and literally transferring responsibility for the horrifying decision to crucify Jesus over to the Jewish leaders so intent on His destruction.

Things we can learn from Pilate's wife about interpreting dreams:

- When prompted to do so by an inspired dream, do

what is necessary, within your stewardship, to inform or warn others about a course of action.
- Act in a timely manner. Had Pilate's wife postponed talking with her husband about this matter, it would have changed the spiritual impact on both of them.
- Take what action you can, even if you cannot completely resolve a problem.

Omer – Ether 9

Omer, a Nephite king, was plagued by family problems that threatened his life; "because of the secret combinations of Akish and his friends, behold, they did overthrow the kingdom of Omer." The Lord was merciful in giving Omer warning, "and also to his sons and to his daughters who did not seek his destruction."

> **3** And the Lord warned Omer in a dream that he should depart out of the land; wherefore Omer departed out of the land with his family, and traveled many days, and came over and passed by the hill of Shim, and came over by the place where the Nephites were destroyed, and from thence eastward, and came to a place which was called Ablom, by the seashore, and there he pitched his tent, and also his sons and his daughters, and all his household, save it were Jared and his family.

Things we can learn from Omer about the interpretation of dreams:

- The Lord will protect his faithful children from spiritual and physical danger, when others make unrighteous choices.
- We must heed the warning to obtain the blessing.

Jacob – Genesis 31

A dream came to Jacob when he was in a tense situation. Jacob was sent by his mother Rebekah to her brother Laban, in the land of Caanan, because Rebekah was concerned about his choosing an appropriate wife. After receiving a blessing from his father, Jacob traveled to his uncle's home. On the way he was given a dream about a ladder reaching into heaven, directing him to extra effort in righteous doing.

When Jacob arrived at his uncle's home, he met Rachel, and loved her right away. Laban, however, insisted that Jacob serve him seven years for the privilege of marrying her. To this Jacob immediately agreed, and the seven years passed quickly. But when the wedding day came, Laban married Jacob to Leah, the older daughter. A week later, he was allowed to marry Rachel as well, but for the price of another seven years' labor managing Laban's flocks of sheep.

At the end of the second seven years, Jacob had four wives and was ready to find some other kind of employment to provide for his family. Dealing with Laban as his boss and father-in-law was becoming more challenging as Laban's sons were becoming jealous of Jacob and his potential share of Laban's estate. Laban's attitude towards Jacob was changing as well; he apparently owed Jacob considerable back wages, but was less able to produce income himself than before.

At this point, Jacob had a dream, in which the rams that mounted the ewes in his flock were "ringstraked, speckled and grisled." An angel of the Lord, who appeared in the dream, pointed out the nature of the rams, and told Jacob to seek those so marked. He also included a reason for the instruction: "for I have seen all that Laban doeth unto thee." Jacob was additionally directed to return to the land of his parents' family.

Having received this information, Jacob offered to divide Laban's flocks over the next couple of seasons, and to receive his wages, by taking the speckled and spotted animals, leaving for Laban the smooth and solid-colored ones, which were more valuable in the current market.

Laban agreed to this arrangement, thinking he would benefit greatly from this transaction, but as it turned out, most of the lambs turned out speckled, and were given to Jacob. Jacob's inspired action was an appropriate and pleasing gesture from Laban's point of view, which helped Jacob to have some peace in the family. The Lord took it from there, causing the majority of the speckled animals to reproduce more abundantly, paying Jacob and setting him up more prosperously in life.

Things we can learn from Jacob about interpreting dreams:
- A dream may inspire a very small change that has big results.
- Trust in the Lord is imperative.

Dreams Offering Comfort

Joseph – Matthew 1

Joseph, a virtuous man, was engaged to Mary, a very special woman, but "before they came together, she was found with child of the Holy Ghost." Joseph's dilemma and pain were intense within the rigid morals of his community. Joseph was distraught over Mary's pregnancy and apparent infidelity. He was of a mind to quietly break the engagement, but a dream came to him that explained the true divine nature of her situation, comforting him greatly.

20 But while he thought on these things, behold, the angel of the Lord appeared unto him in a dream, saying, Joseph, thou son of David, fear not to take unto thee Mary thy wife: for that which is conceived in her is of the Holy Ghost.

Joseph was blessed with tremendous comfort at this difficult time. Despite the embarrassment of an unexpected pregnancy, which hinted of error on his and Mary's part, Joseph was directed to proceed in faith with the planned marriage, knowing in full of their innocence of wrongdoing. His role was clarified, and he was given new responsibility as guardian of his Lord.

Things we can learn from Joseph about the interpretation of dreams:

- A prayer for divine help will clarify understanding, often in the form of a dream.
- Things are not always what they appear to be. Sometimes things are much, much better than we expect.
- An inspired dream, properly understood, will help you grasp and follow truth, despite intense opposition.

Solomon – 1 Kings 3

When David died and Solomon became king over Israel, he was overwhelmed with the responsibility. One night the Lord appeared to him in a dream, and said to him "Ask what I shall give thee." Solomon answered:

7 And now, O Lord my God, thou hast made thy servant king instead of David my father: and I am but a little child: I know not how to go out or come in.

8 And thy servant is in the midst of thy people which thou hast chosen, a great people, that cannot be numbered nor counted for multitude.

9 Give therefore thy servant an understanding heart to judge thy people, that I may discern between good and bad: for who is able to judge this thy so great a people?

The Lord was pleased that Solomon asked for wisdom to rule well, instead of something selfish:

11 And God said unto him, Because thou hast asked this thing, and hast not asked for thyself long life; neither hast asked riches for thyself, nor hast asked the life of thine enemies; but hast asked for thyself understanding to discern judgment;

12 Behold, I have done according to thy words: lo, I have given thee a wise and an understanding heart; so that there was none like thee before thee, neither after thee shall any arise like unto thee.

13 And I have also given thee that which thou hast not asked, both riches, and honour: so that there shall not be any among the kings like unto thee all thy days.

Solomon was given far more than he asked for, because his heart was set on doing that which would bless the people, not on obtaining things that would glorify himself. He was willing to partner with the Lord in working righteousness.

Things we can learn from Solomon about the interpretation of dreams:

- A messenger may come in an inspired dream, bringing important instruction or wisdom.
- One of the ways the Lord communicates with us is through inspired dreams.
- An unselfish heart opens us to greater wisdom from above.

Section 2:
The Interpretation Process

The prophet Joel described events preceding the coming of Jesus Christ, when God would begin to pour out his Spirit on all flesh. Visions and dreams were to be part of that outpouring. (Joel 2: 27-29)

In the New Testament, Peter explained the amazing signs and presence of the Spirit on the Day of Pentecost. He mentioned Joel's prophetic words, commenting on their fulfillment (in part) on that day:

Acts 2:16 But this is that which was spoken by the prophet Joel;

17 And it shall come to pass in the last days, saith God, I will pour out of my Spirit upon all flesh: and your sons and your daughters shall prophesy, and your young men shall see visions, and your old men shall dream dreams:

18 And on my servants and on my handmaidens I will pour out in those days of my Spirit; and they shall prophesy:

We are in the days prophesied by Joel and Peter. Many people in and out of the Church experience dreams that have message and meaning. It is to our advantage to learn how such dreams work. Bridging the distance from scripture time to real time is not so daunting as it might appear at first. Just remember the lessons you have learned in Section 1.

Step 1:
Preparing to Interpret Your Dreams

Dream interpretations do not come into a spiritual vacuum. Preparation and humility are necessary to enjoy the benefits of a true interpretation. Any other kind of interpretation will be without the power and insight only the Lord can provide.

Spiritual preparation, including obedience to God's laws, prayer, scripture study and selfless service to others, is essential. At times, a small child will have dreams regarding their family circumstances when their parents are not walking in a spiritually receptive path.

Being your best is an ongoing process, with varying states of success or failure at living the way you know you should. It is an ongoing process. Do what you can to repent of errors and move forward. Daily prayer and Gospel study will go far in preparing you for inspired dreams. Avoid harsh criticism of self or others, but hold yourself accountable to what you know is right. Focus on being honest and humble, yet positive with yourself. You are infinitely loved and cherished by your Heavenly Father, who is anxious to bless you and help you learn.

Prepare Continually:

Four types of preparation are vital to effectively interpreting your dreams:
- Your **physical readiness** is essential to remembering and recording your dream.
- Your **spiritual readiness** will enable you to see beyond the physical, helping you to understand your dream more fully.
- Your **emotional and mental readiness** will allow you to avoid errors in judgment as you prepare your interpretation.
- Your degree of **humility and being teachable** will allow you to reap the full intended blessings of your dream.

Consider your physical readiness

You might find and use a special journal and pen that you keep handy right by your bed for recording dreams. If dreams come in the middle of the night, it is to your benefit to be willing to get up and record the dream, or at least lie in bed and write what you can remember of it. It doesn't have to look nice or make sense just yet, you just need the details written down someplace so you can return and piece it all back together. You can do the analysis later.

Consider your spiritual readiness

A simple prayer immediately when you awaken from a dream, asking for help in remembering, discerning and interpreting it, will go far in helping with your process of understanding and correctly interpreting the dream. Sincere prayer immediately after a dream opens your mind to any assistance that may come, but it does not take the place of the hard work of discerning the truth from everything else in a dream. Most dreams should not be taken literally. Your ability to interpret dreams is affected by the choices you make daily. Be the wisest, best, purest vessel you know how to be. Repent as you need to. Remember that repentance is like bathing, best applied daily or nearly so. Do the best you can, and let the

Lord make up the difference between that and perfection. Don't condemn or criticize yourself. Simply move forward. Avoid occult practices, evil atmospheres or evil spirits, and people, media, or other influences dwelling on or dealing with such things. Protect yourself from the deception and destruction they invite. Consider the example of Saul in 1 Samuel 28, when he sought the advice of a witch and brought disappointing error and spiritual blockage upon himself.

Avoid being caught up in the dreams or interpretations of others, especially those who do not have worthy stewardship over your welfare. The dream came to you, so you are the interpreter of it, ultimately. Zechariah 10:2 warns of those who may lie or deceive regarding dreams and visions, seeking gain or undue influence. Guard your power to choose carefully.

Consider your emotional and mental readiness

Your mental and emotional lens through which you view life colors your understanding of dreams. Dreams are an invitation to grow and nurture your understanding, process grief and trauma, and recover emotional and mental health, but they can also be a means of simply releasing feelings.

Jeremiah 29 suggests that true doctrine takes precedence over the interpretation of any dream. Be wise in your actions, and do not let a simple dream overwhelm your common sense and the love and wisdom of God and His chosen servants. Consider what is going on in your life that may unduly influence your dreams, and judge wisely the importance of dreams produced in a frenzied, depressed, lovesick or grieving state. Perhaps proportionally scale back the importance and influence of such dreams in your decision-making.

The following analogy in pertains more to having faith in the Lord's deliverance from those who fight against Zion than to dreams - but it has an important message for those currently troubled by an unbalanced mental or emotional state, and perhaps frightening or upsetting dreams resulting from it.

2 Nephi 27:3 And all the nations that fight against Zion, and that distress her, shall be as a dream of a night vision; yea, it shall be unto them, even as unto a hungry man which dreameth, and behold he eateth but he awaketh and his soul is empty; or like unto a thirsty man which dreameth, and behold he drinketh but he awaketh and behold he is faint, and his soul hath appetite; yea, even so shall the multitude of all the nations be that fight against Mount Zion.

In short, dreams of themselves don't amount to anything. What matters is the action we choose to take as a result. It's OK to say, "It's just a dream" and forget it. Remember that you are an agent, a person with the power to choose – not just an object to be acted upon.

Consider your humility and ability to be teachable

Inspired dreams do not come on command. Like other inspiration, they come on the Lord's terms, and in His way. Dreams are more symbolic, however, to preserve your agency. They require more time and effort to understand, but can yield great treasures of wisdom and comfort.

Dreams can be humbling. You may be invited to examine less-attractive aspects of your character. Do so gladly. Job offers a wonderful perspective on dreams as correction or instruction from the Lord:

> **Job 33:12** ...I will answer thee, that God is greater than man.
> **13** Why dost thou strive against him? for he giveth not account of any of his matters.
> **14** For God speaketh once, yea twice, yet man perceiveth it not.
> **15** In a dream, in a vision of the night, when deep sleep falleth upon men, in slumberings upon the bed;
> **16** Then he openeth the ears of men, and sealeth their instruction,
> **17** That he may withdraw man from his purpose, and hide pride from man.
> **18** He keepeth back his soul from the pit, and his life from perishing by the sword.

Nephi's example of humility and being teachable in 1 Nephi 15 contrasts sharply with Laman and Lemuel's casual disregard of their prophet father's message. Nephi's willingness to inquire of the Lord led to a detailed understanding of his father Lehi's dream that blesses readers of the Book of Mormon to this day. He pondered and prayed about the details of the dream, and gained important instruction from the Lord. Nephi's humility blessed him with the ability to teach his brothers and family as well.

In Summary:

- Be willing to record your dreams.
- Be willing to listen to messages from the Lord, even ones you don't like, and try to see things from His point of view.
- Exercise your faith in obedience. Remember He has your eternal happiness and well-being at heart and loves you more than anyone on Earth possibly can.
- Consider how honest you are being with yourself, even as you take your circumstances into consideration.
- Be cautious in sharing your dreams with others. Remember also that the dream and its interpretation are centered in your own life and stewardship. Be wise.

Understand your role

Dreams are one way that God reveals His will to men and women on earth. Even children may receive inspired dreams. Not all dreams are revelations, however. Inspired dreams are the fruit of faith in and obedience to divine law.

Gospel Topics and Bible Dictionary at lds.org present several definitions important to consider in the interpretation and sharing of dreams. These definitions clarify the importance of agency and order in revelation. It is natural, when our dreams involve others, or are especially concerning in nature, to want to share them. However, it is imperative that we respect and honor our own agency and stewardship, and that of others, in doing so.

Agency:
"Agency is the ability and privilege God gives us to choose and to act for ourselves."

Stewardship:
Stewardship is defined as a "Responsibility to administer or attend to the assignments one receives in a Church calling, or to take care of those things with which we are blessed from God, including families, neighbors, and even temporal blessings. Stewardship is spiritual oversight, and responsibility to inform. It is not and never should have any degree of compulsion

or dominance. Stewardship is a responsibility to see to the needs of, make suggestions to or teach a person... Again, it is important to remember that there is no compulsion or dominance implied in this right."

Varying degrees of stewardship, of course, are implied in family relationships and in that of a friend. You have a degree of stewardship for your own children, grandchildren, parents, siblings and other family members. Others who may have an interchange of stewardship with you include neighbors, teachers, ministering brothers or sisters and leaders in a particular assignment.

Revelation:
"Communication from God to his children on earth. Revelation may come through the Light of Christ and the Holy Ghost by way of inspiration, visions, dreams, or visits by angels."

There is order in the receiving of revelation:
"In the Lord's Church the First Presidency and the Council of the Twelve are prophets, seers, and revelators to the Church and to the world. In addition, every person may receive personal revelation for his own benefit. *It is contrary to the laws of God for any person to receive revelation for those higher in authority*" (italics added).

How do these concepts apply to interpreting dreams?

The symbolism of your dream is given to YOUR understanding. The presence of others in your dream is significant only in light of their meaning in your life or their relationship to you. Sharing your dream is up to you, and others may find edification or learning from your experience, but only according to their own desire to seek it.

The dream is an invitation to you to act or change. YOU make choices about the importance or influence of the dream, and what it means to you. You have the option of completely disregarding any dream that comes to you. This may be a good idea when faced with frightening or nightmarish dreams.

Not every dream merits full analysis. Some dreams may be the result of indigestion, illness or spiritual attack. Prayerfully decide what to take from each one. You may elect to take nothing and move on with your day. You may choose to spend time recording and analyzing a dream. The choice is yours. The decision and responsibility of what to DO about any interpretation is fully yours as well.

Allow time for pondering and reflection when you determine that a dream needs interpretation. This will probably necessitate writing down the dream and taking time to think about it.

Inspired dreams, like other revelation, can be understood from different perspectives, in different layers. It is beneficial to you to look at your dream from several angles. What you understand from a dream on the day the dream comes to you may be quite different from what you see in it twenty years later. You may not fully understand the dream for years – but the time and effort spent on an inspired dream will be richly rewarding and eminently worthwhile, both now and in the future.

STEP 2:
RECORD THE DREAM & YOUR PERSPECTIVE

Your memory of a dream decreases the longer you wait to write it down. Once you write a dream, however, it become more permanent, and it is much easier to analyze objectively. Consider keeping something by your bed to record the dream.

When you go to record a dream, start by working chronologically, quickly recording the main happenings of the dream, along with every detail you can, and feelings at each stage of the dream. Record colors, scenery, associations with your real life, etc. A tiny detail, such as the unexpected color of an item, may be the key to unlocking the interpretation of the dream.

Sometimes you may have forgotten parts of the dream, but that is all right; record what you can remember, and glean what you can from that. You might need to come back to this step several times, as you remember additional details.

Sometimes a dream will come with a spiritual impression, such as words of counsel or warning, or you may have some immediate insight into the meaning that relates to what is going on in your life.

You may see associations to what has occupied

your thoughts lately. Often these are only part of the interpretation.

There are a lot of dreams that leave you wondering "What in the world???" Write those down. There will always be a deeper and more significant layer of meaning.

Take the time to look deeper.

As you write down details of your dream, be sure to include the following:
- Note details of your location and how that changes through the dream.
- Note distinguishing characteristics of people, places and animals in your dream, and their words, actions and attitudes. Note especially anything of unusual size, shape, color, texture, etc.
- Note the sequence of events.
- Note colors that appear, even if you only notice in passing - but especially if they are not typical of real life.
- Note feelings that occur to you as you proceed through the dream, and any associations you may remember with individuals or places from your past.
- Note any messages that come to you as you awaken. These will be an important part of the interpretation.
- Pay attention to the symbols, both individually and

collectively. In any dream that you deem worthy of your consideration, every detail has significance in understanding the dream's full message.

When God communicates with you and touches your heart, He uses things you can fully understand. He is the Master Teacher. The process of pondering promotes additional learning and teaches us to look at things the way God does.

When faced with a very perplexing dream, consider the possibility that God is trying to express something to you that is so far out of your current realm of knowledge that He must piece it together for you, like an intricate quilt, using bits of things that you do understand. He is infinitely able to do this! Once you have pondered the dream you will be more prepared to comprehend the idea He is trying to communicate to you.

STEP 3:
UNDERSTAND THE SIGNIFICANCE OF SYMBOLS

Why symbols?

The Lord has always used symbols to teach his children. In its most basic form, symbolism means that a visible or concrete object is used to represent a more abstract idea or feeling. Dreams, by nature, are highly symbolic.

Symbolism abounds in the Scriptures. The rainbow was a symbol of God's promise to Noah that He would not flood the entire Earth again. Symbolic patterns abound in worship and in the poetic language of Scripure. Consider the original language in which the Book of Mormon was written: reformed Egyptian. Hieroglyphic characters are symbolic of entire ideas, not just phonetic sounds; each character can carry more meaning in less space than the longer series of characters that form the same idea in other languages. When one is engraving on gold plates, space matters.

Similarly, the Lord through the Holy Spirit can communicate multiple layers of original, inspired thought and understanding to our minds – instantly - by using symbols that have meaning to us individually. Dreams may at first seem perplexing, and take considerable time to unravel, but they can contain worlds of information in just a short space.

It is estimated that the conscious mind uses only 10 percent of the brain's capacity on an everyday basis. Dreams come from the other 90 percent, the subconscious and unconsciousparts, which remember, make connections, and create through the influence of the Spirit of God.

An inspired dream is custom-designed by the Lord, using your constantly-operating subconscious and unconscious mind, to convey an important message to you. Your ordinary dreams will be similarly symbolic, as your deep, divinely-designed mind operates and communicates to your conscious mind though symbols, logic and feelings.

Endowed From On High, a Church handbook designed for Temple preparation, offers some interesting insight into the importance of symbols in the Lord's communication with us:
- Symbols can help us remember important things.
- Symbols can teach us abstract truths that might be hard to learn in other ways.
- Symbols can represent feelings.
- Symbols can teach different principles according to our personal readiness to learn.

Understanding the importance and efficiency of symbols makes it easy to see why our dreams are so symbolic. Even when there is a lot to understand, the meaning can be packed concisely into a short dream. Taking the time to fully unpack that dream defines the process of interpretation. The Lord is efficient yet personalized in His communication with His children.

The Endowed From On High manual also states:
"The Lord reveals truth to those who are spiritually ready to understand it. Those who receive truth with faith and obedience continue to receive more truth. Those who are not spiritually prepared and who fail to receive truth or receive it with a doubtful heart will gradually lose the truth they have. Stories with symbols present truth in such a way that those who are spiritually prepared understand the meaning of the symbols. Those who are not prepared do not understand the meaning."

The symbolism of dreams is intended to preserve your divine gift of agency, or your power to choose - and also to allow you to benefit from the dream even as you grow in wisdom, understanding and spiritual capacity. Sometimes the settings and characters of your dream themselves are strange and surreal. Remember not to take them literally or at least immediately at face value. Again, look deeper.

Each component of your dream is a symbol that carries meaning having significance to you in your life and calling to memory from your own experiences.

Each may represent something being brought to your attention, particularly hidden or forgotten characteristics or associations. Dreaming of doing something or going somewhere does not automatically mean you are being instructed to do that thing, or foretelling some action. It may only be intended to evoke feelings regarding that place or action, perhaps as part of a larger theme of instruction.

Look up ideas from a dream dictionary, considering all the symbols in the dream, and where you are in your life right now. What is the dream trying to tell you? This step is where you try to make sense of everything all together, and consider what meaning or action it suggests to you.

The suggested action will likely be different for every dream. You don't have to come up with something right away. Just let your mind percolate on it. It may take some time, but you can think about the dream while you are driving, doing chores or other tasks that don't require a lot of active thought.

There are several useful and free dream dictionaries online. One good one I use frequently is www.dreambible.com, but there are numerous others. A dream dictionary should be considered a supplement to your own experience and understanding of a symbol, as are the interpretations of anyone you share the dream with.

Remember to look for symbolism, especially regarding sensitive, sacred or private topics, and consider various meanings of what happens in the dream, and how each can help you move forward. With practice, you will be able to discern which interpretations don't really apply to you, and see those that do pertain to your situation.

STEP 4:
PRAYERFULLY CHOOSE YOUR INTERPRETATION

Now that you have written down the details and considered symbolic meaning, prayerfully look at the dream all together again, with all you have gleaned, including your knowledge and feelings.

Pray for help in discerning correct interpretations, as well as recognizing the overall importance of the dream to you personally. You will need to sift through various possible meanings for each symbol. Take your time and consider each possibility.

If you are willing to act or change, as necessary, you will benefit from your understanding of the dream, as it is an invitation to progress. A correct interpretation of your dream's details will feel different from other, irrelevant interpretations. It will be more calm, positive and concrete. It will feel better than the incorrect possibilities. Think of it as gold mining – you have to sift through a number of possibilities to locate the nuggets of truth. After a while, the correct meanings will stand out like bright color against a gray wall, and take on an overall shape and meaning that will elevate your understanding. When you find truths, make a note. Some dreams are more important than others, but a grain of meaning can be extracted from any dream.

Consider the following types of dreams:

Ordinary dreams

Ordinary dreams are forgettable, gone nearly as soon as you awake. An ordinary dream leaves no unusual feeling in your mind. However, writing every dream can be a good exercise in interpretation, dealing with their milder feelings in practice, to evaluate them for what they are worth. Some little lesson or insight will turn up.

Odd dreams

Odd dreams have more perplexing features or unusual associations that beg a further personal examination, and perhaps a laugh when shared with family or friends.

Odd dreams can mean you have some kind of emotion to resolve, or there is something your subconscious has figured out for you and is trying to communicate to your conscious mind. It may also be a spiritual message to you from God.

A dream may or may not have spiritual significance, but prayerful consideration will always help you discern and decipher it. At any rate, it will be an interesting exercise. Usually some kind of needed change, and the reason for it, will become apparent to you by evaluating the dream. It may be only an attitude shift, but remember that great changes can come through small means (Alma 37:6-7).

A woman who was preparing for baptism found that the weight of her financial obligations prevented her from meeting her baptism date. Her health was poor, and she was concerned about living long enough to accept baptism in this life. She was behind in her taxes, and living so close to the line that, despite careful budgeting and absolutely minimal spending, she had only a dollar left at the end of the month, and no savings at all. She felt completely unable to pay tithing, and without that commitment she could not be approved for baptism. She prayed for help in knowing what to do.

The next morning, he woman awoke from a dream that she felt was instruction from God. In the dream, she was driving her car, and had just crossed a bridge. She came to a stop. On the right was a large house, but it had no door. On the left were flowers and a graveyard. Straight ahead was a road, and at the end was the Salt Lake Temple, where she was headed. However, the road before her was blocked by impassable, deep ditches and road construction. People were working to complete it. As she awoke, it was made clear to her that she was to wait there in her car until the road was passable.

She decided to continue attending her meetings, and wait for the Lord to open the way. Peace and a feeling of calmness accompanied this decision. The time eventually came within a few months when she was able to move forward with her baptism, and manage her financial obligations.

Terrifying dreams

Terrifying dreams are not unusual, especially if you are unwell mentally, physically or emotionally. They can be brought on by trauma, real or remembered, even imagined. A feeling of terror or fear can be an indication of spiritual illness or attack. Resist the urge to believe the dream literally, and seek calming, spiritually uplifting surroundings. Write the dream down, so the emotions of it are not so preeminent in your mind. You need to be able to think clearly. Then proceed with your evaluation and interpretation, if you want to. Such a dream can be some kind of warning. However, you may choose to dismiss the dream outright if it appears to be of evil nature. You always have that choice.

Disturbing dreams

Disturbing dreams may feature unpleasant images, associations or emotions that conflict with your values or run against your usual practices. Dreams are a reflection of your entire human experience, not just the public parts of it. Disturbing dreams may be an unpleasant merging of your public and private self, or involve subject matter you prefer not to record. This is ok. The dream still has value, perhaps more than you realize. You can still go through the evaluation and interpretation process. While you may feel uncomfortable writing the dream down, you can choose to use abbreviations or otherwise code your writing, or put it in a secure place, so you can still distance yourself from the dream a bit and evaluate it.

Disturbing dreams may leave you feeling ashamed or confused, especially if your values are close-held and high, but as you look at them honestly, there may be a grain of truth in it all. Look at the dream objectively; disturbing dreams can be a warning to you of possible danger ahead if you persist in your current course. Be grateful for any warning or correction implied, and recognize and remember that a dream is not the same as an action. Look for the symbolism; sexual dreams may simply indicate that you see qualities you admire in someone else now developing in yourself, for example. Deal directly and honestly with the emotions the dream evokes in you. Look at disturbing dreams as an invitation to improve your attitude or understanding, and to make positive choices in your life. Again, you are free to simply disregard the dream if you feel it is of evil intent.
Example: A woman had a dream of herself in bed with her pastor, in a dark room with curtains closed. When

she found herself there in the dream, she was distressed, and immediately got up, and walked to the window. She parted the curtains, and outside was a beautiful summer day, with wonderful corn growing tall in the garden. When she woke up, she felt like there was something to this dream, but the associations of course bothered her quite a bit. She was happily married, and had no romantic ideas about the man in her dream, although she did admire some of his professional skills.

As she interpreted the dream, she came to realize that the message indicated that she was already acquiring professional skills that were on par with his, and that she could use to better effect as she focused on her own blessings and relationships, and less on his skills. The interpretation was far less disturbing than the dream, but there was definite instruction and wisdom that gave her confidence to move forward in her life.

Momentous dreams

Momentous dreams are remarkable, clear, and unforgettable. They resonate with importance, and may seem to be a pivot upon which your whole future life turns .They seem to affect the way in which you will make all future decisions. Momentous dreams may come only once, perhaps in a blinding flash, or be repeated so often that you feel they must have some significance. They may just leave you awakening with a feeling of their deep importance, regardless of the subject matter of the dream.

Momentous dreams calmly change you into someone different than you were before. They come with a peaceful feeling that points to the truth resonating in the dream. These are the dreams most likely to contain revelation, and perhaps warning, but remember that they are symbolic, and not necessarily literal. The meaning of even a prophetic dream will involve your choices far more than the choices of others. This is important to remember.

Step 5:
Access the Atonement of Jesus Christ: "Help Thou Mine Unbelief"

When dealing with upsetting dreams, or with interpretations that seem overwhelming to you, remember that there is power beyond your own upon which you can call. Exercise your faith in the Atonement of Jesus Christ to work through the dream more positively. Remember to keep an eternal perspective.

The object of receiving revelation is to align your will with God's, not the other way around. Exercising faith in Him, and submitting our will to his, allows Him to supplement our mortal (and imperfect) efforts with his infinite love, power and wisdom, opening the way to miracles according to His will. Doing so allows you to gain new understanding, and make needed changes in your attitude or actions; you will enjoy wider perspective, divine protection and personal growth.

A young father begged Jesus to help his young son, who was afflicted by an evil spirit that threatened the boy's destruction and death.
The father said to Jesus, "But if thou canst do any thing, have compassion on us, and help us."
Jesus said unto him, "If thou canst believe, all things are possible to him that believeth."
"And straightway the father of the child cried out, and said with tears, Lord, I believe; help thou mine unbe-

lief."

Jesus then rebuked the evil spirit and charged it to "come out of him, and enter no more into him. And the spirit cried, and rent him sore, and came out of him." (Mark 9:14-29)

    Belief in the miraculous power of the Atonement of Jesus Christ empowers individuals who lack the faith to move to the next level when faced with what God asks of them. Even if only a desire to believe is the best we can come up with, and we allow that desire to work in us, the Lord can magnify that desire and work miracles. (Alma 32:27)

    Each of us has found or will find ourselves at our mortal limit, whether physically, emotionally, mentally or spiritually. The priceless gift of the Atonement allows us, when we have done all we can, to place our trust in the all-powerful nature of the Lord. When we have done all we can, He will supply the strength we need to believe, to carry on, to change our lives, or to change our perspective. When we truly desire to see as He sees, and give our will over to Him, His power and grace will rest upon us, and miracles happen.

    The sacred power of God's grace relates to our attitudes and the understanding of our dreams as well. When the process of interpreting a dream reveals that I am in error on some point, or that I should take a certain course of action, for example, my natural reaction can be somewhat less than enthusiastic, or even negative. But if I, in prayer, sincerely ask for the power of the Atonement in overcoming my mortal self, power is gently given: an attitude shifts, my perspective widens to include God's, and my fears are laid to rest. This power is beyond anything of mine, but it strengthens and clarifies my judgment. It helps me get out of my own way in moving forward.

True progress is what it's all about, isn't it? God bless you in your journey.

C. L. Hale

www.ingramcontent.com/pod-product-compliance
Lightning Source LLC
Chambersburg PA
CBHW071117030426
42336CB00013BA/2118